In The Missouri Woods

Mary Worrell Hudson

IN THE
MISSOURI WOODS.

MRS. J. K. HUDSON.

1905

TO A LOVER OF NATURE

MY FRIEND

MATHILDA WILLITTS KINGMAN.

Gravois Creek.

*And out of the ground made the Lord
God to grow every tree that is pleasant to
the sight.   —Genesis.*

*Let him whose heart is beauty wise,
Now on the greenwood feast his eyes—
Full green-bedecked and merry.
          —Frederick, Count Leiningen.
               A. D., 1189.*

The Three Notches.

SPRINGTIME IN THE HEART
OF MISSOURI.

Where is the poet who can sing the beauties
of these hills and vales? There are loftier heights
and broader streams, more grandeur and awe-
someness, but here beauty is spread over all. I
have never yet read a single poem that described
in full the wild-woods springtime in the heart of
Missouri. No place in which in my limited trav-
els I have ever seen spring come on compares
with this in the quantity and variety of its wild
flowers. Perhaps there is a reason for this. For
generations of men the timber throughout several counties hereabouts has been culled for
railroad ties, so that the vast forests are
really forests of comparatively small trees.
When an oak tree is large enough to "square
a tie," its span of life is run. Everyone who
is in the least woods-wise knows that of all
places in the world, wild flowers love an abandoned "clearing," where the stumps stand thick,
and the logs lie rotting in the mold, and the wild

vines run riot, and the blackberry bushes tangle
things up so that the wayfarer is soon discour-
aged. The Missouri woods is not an abandoned
clearing, but it is better, it is all the time being
cleared and all the time growing up. It is a
shady "open," full of abandoned tree tops, and
all that portion of the aspiring young tree that
was not carried away in a "tie." The ground is
disturbed just enough to encourage the flowers,
and they move up in close, beautiful battalions
wherever the sun shines through. Just here, the
little Ozarks begin, the prairie suddenly dropping
off into what the hill people call the "brakes."
Rugged ups and downs, seamed with mineral-
stained rocks, and divided by little cascad-
ing, crystal streams, whose margins are fringed
with stonecrop and spiderwort and toadflax and
ferns. Ferns drape all the northside rocks and
and banks and ledges, and cluster in the little
cañons and valleys, and moss is everywhere. The
roots on the shady side of a tree are covered
throughout their sometimes long and tortuous
length with a velvet mantle, and in certain nooks
that one comes upon every few paces there are
beds of dappled green large enough for a whole
troup of fairies to dance upon, or for a tired mortal to recline upon at his ease. "The woods" in

central and southern Missouri does not mean a
grove, or a wood-lot, or a rambling stretch of
wood land along the banks of a stream, but miles
and miles of woods that has never been anything
else since the glacial period, or at least not since
the Louisiana purchase. And yet it is not the
primeval forest. The natives call it "second
growth" timber, but it is more nearly the tenth
growth, probably, since the original emigrants
from St. Louis began cutting logs for forts and
houses, and later for rails and ties. There is only
here and there an ancient giant, and he only escaped because he is hollow-hearted or deformed
or soft of fibre.

The monarch of the lowlands is the sycamore,
that stands many feet above all other trees,
stretching long, white arms athwart the blue
sky. Undisturbed because it is not worth cutting down, this picturesque tree grows to great
size and dies of old age. Even then the giant
skeleton still stands, bleaching whiter each year
and forming a landmark that breaks the monot-
ony of the beautiful green rythm and serves the
purpose of the occasional odd measure which the
true poet and artist must use. Standing here on
the high divide which separates two noble rivers,
the Missouri and the Osage, the prospect is one

to awaken all the poetic fancies and memories of a life time. Fold upon fold, hill against hill, the banks of tender green fade away to the southward into the purplish distance. As evening comes on, thin clouds, white and amethystine, rise out of the intervening valleys and set the hills farther apart and give them greater difference of height and contour, until the last one on the dim horizon seems far removed. When morning dispels the valley mists the hills draw together again, and you wonder what has become of the rocks and streams and highways that you followed yesterday. But they are there, hidden from view only while you stand on the heights. Suddenly you think of Chatterton's sweet song:

"When Spring came dancing on a floweret bed,
    Dight in green raiment of a changing kind,
The leaves of hawthorne budding on his head,
    And wythe primrose crouching to the wynde;
Then did the shepherd his long alban spread
    Upon the green banks as he danced around,
Whilst the sweet flowerets nodded on his head,
    And his fair lambs were scattered on the ground,
Against his foot the brooklet ran along,
Which strolleth round the vale to hear his joyous song."

And you know that the brook still strolleth, and ever, ever will.

There is an Indian legend, belonging to the great tribe of Osages, once monarchs of all this region, that tells the story of the spring colors. It runs like this:

"Once, long before there were men in the world, all the earth was covered with ice and snow.

"White and frozen lay the rivers and the sea; white and frozen lay the plains. The mountains stood tall and dead, like ghosts in white gowns. There was no color but white in all the world excepting the sky, and it was almost black. At night the stars looked through it like angry eyes.

"Then God sent the spring down into the world—the spring with red lips and curling yellow hair.

"In his arms he bore sprays of apple blossoms and the first flowers—crocus, anemones and violets, red, pink, blue, purple, violet and yellow.

"The first animal to greet the spring, was the white rabbit. The spring dropped a red crocus on his head, and ever since then all white rabbits have red eyes.

"Then the spring dropped a blue violet on a white bird, the first bird to greet the spring, and that is the way the bluebird was made. Ever since then it is the first bird to arrive when the spring comes down from heaven.

"So the spring went through the world. Wherever he tossed the leaves from his fragrant burden, the earth became green. He tossed the blossoms on the frozen seas and the ice melted and the fish became painted with all the tints of his flowers. That is the way the trout and the minnows and the salmon were rainbow-colored.

"Only the high mountains would not bow to the spring. So their summits remain white and dead, for they would let the spring paint only their sides.

"The snow owls and the white geese and the polar bears fled from the spring, so they, too, remain white to this day."

The conceit is a pretty one, for where is the magician who can show the spectrum in all its rays like unto the springtime? Just now the wind-flower and the violet blow side by side in lavish profusion, but the frail anemone will be the first to disappear and hide its dainty head until another April comes to scatter pink and lavender on favored spots of earth like this.

THE WOODS IN MARCH.

What a comfort to lovers of nature and amateur observers of nature's ways is Mr. John Burrough's article in the March *Century*, entitled "On Humanizing the Animals."

I had begun to despair of my own powers of seeing things after reading two or three volumes of "Nature Studies," particularly animal-nature studies.. I have never seen any mother birds teaching their young ones to fly, nor caught any song birds teaching the score of the tribe, note by note, to the young birds. Others—those, too, who believed themselves competent to write books on the subject—have seen these and many more wonderful things not yet detected by John Burroughs. He says of these people that "they are incapable of disinterested observation, which means that they are incapable of observation at all in its true sense." Now, we can all go on enjoying the birds of the air and the tiny beasts of the field and wood, though we have never chanced upon one of their private schools of locomotion, music, or breakfast foods. Their knowledge of how to do all these things, Mr. Burroughs claims, is instinctive, and he thinks it is of vital importance to the continuance of the species that it should be. "If it were a matter of instruction or acquired knowledge, how precarious it would be!" he says. The wise naturestudents may discuss that point with Mr. Burroughs if they like, but my enjoyment of the statement lies in the fact that I feel justified in never having found an animal college in the woods. But there is another idea in this interesting article on humanizing the animals more startling still.

There are those among us, "takin' notes," too, who believe that the next step in the evolution of the mind of man will be telepathy—that is, telepathy for all. Here comes John Burroughs saying that he can only account for the "community of mind" in flocks and herds by something analogous to telepathy. He is convinced that movements of gregarious animals are not guided or controlled by any system of language or signs, but by "a community of mind among them in a sense that there is not among men." Continuing, he says that "the pressure of great danger seems to develop in a degree this community of mind and feeling among men.

Under strong excitement we revert more or less
to the animal state, and are ruled by instinct.
It may well be that telepathy—the power to
project one's mental or emotional state so as to
impress a friend at a distance—is a power which
we have carried over from our remote animal
ancestors."

What do the mind readers, and the new-
thought projectors think of that! Telepathy,
according to Mr. Burroughs, then, must be a
well-nigh lost instinct rather than a new power
about to be acquired by the whole human
family.

What would we plain plodders do without
the scientists to turn things topsy-turvy once
in a while? It is much more entertaining as
well as profitable to think forwards awhile and
then backwards for a time. But without a
John Burroughs to call a halt on the romantic
nature scribblers many of us would have unwit-
tingly followed their lead, it is so fascinating.
This true woodsman says: "The tendency to
sentimentalize nature has, in our time, largely
taken the place of the old tendency to demonize
and spiritize it." What a wide and comprehen-
sive view those few words afford of all the nature
writing that has ever been done, from the fables

of Æsop down to Ernest Thompson Seton's
charming story of "Wahb."

A long time getting to the woods? Yes.
But who would not rather wait for John Burroughs than go to the woods without him?
The President of the United States was proud
to wait for him and see the Yellowstone Park
under his tutelage.

The woods that I go to is mostly hillside
and brookside—just the kind of woods that
any one would choose if choice were given.

To see the very first signs of spring one must
select a ravine that runs east and west, and then
look at the north bank on which the sun shines
all day. There may be a soft blanket, or at
least a patchwork quilt, of snow over the slope
on the south side of the brook for many days
after life is beginning to peep forth on the sunny
side, and it is a wonder how things over there in
the shade ever catch up.

The birds know that spring has come and
that the sap is running in the trees, for the sap-
sucker is to be heard on every side boring smooth
round holes through the bark, and finding a fat
grub every now and then as well as plenty of
sweet sap. There are so many kinds of wood-
peckers, big and little and of many colors. I

An Oak Opening.

undertook to assort them one day in Professor Goss's "History of the Birds of Kansas," which lies open on my desk most of the time at this season of the year, but I found that, like the little girl from Topeka, I did not care for their "botanical" names. They are more interesting as "speckled," "red-headed," "golden-winged," "ivory-billed," etc. It is amazing to see in what a regular row some of these hard-working birds will girdle a tree with holes, sometimes two or three rows, one but a few inches above another. If you get near enough it is easy to see that the tail-feathers are pointed and stiff as well as the bill, and that in climbing a tree, and especially while at work drilling, these sharp feather ends are thrust into the unevennesses of the bark, and thus serve as a partial support or brace. Just after our coming upon the scene had frightened away a beautiful bird with bands of black and white on its wings and tail and a brilliant crimson cap, a before-handed butterfly came fluttering up from among the dead leaves on the ground and alighted beside one of the woodpecker holes which was moist with sap and proceeded to drink its fill, just as if the feast had been prepared specially for him.

If you are looking for ferns the first thing in

the spring you will not find them. It is cold
yet in the places where ferns grow, and the new
fronds are not visible. In sheltered spots there
are yet green leaves left over from last year, but
they are not fresh and bright, and only serve to
mark the spot where more may be expected
after a while. If you are not familiar with the
woods, and particularly if you are not ac-
quainted with a mossy woods, such as may be
found in the heart of Missouri, the thing that
will surprise you most in March is the moss. It
has been growing all winter, and is as green as
emerald. In contrast with the many green varieties, there is a beautiful gray moss that is as
silvery as the pendant Spanish moss of a more
southern latitude on the cypress and live-oak
when it is fresh grown, and velvety to the touch.
All that moss needs is moisture in the ground,
humidity in the air, and shade at least a part of
the time. It holds its own with more complex
and apparently hardier vegetation all over the
world. There is no country, no climate, no alti-
tude in which it does not flourish. When it
dries out in summer, high up on the barren
rock ledges and turns almost brown, a single
shower will revive it. The cells and sectional
tubes of its stems drink up the refreshing water
and begin to turn green in an hour. We gath-

ered beautiful green moss for Christmas decoration, and it has been growing greener ever since. Another simple form of growth that thrived all winter is the lichen. The little plantations that were set out on the rocks and old logs last fall have spread and enlarged until now there are great patches of the crumpled velvet in the most delicate shades of greenish-white and whitish-pink, gray and yellow and brown, with here and there a black lining or a purple facing. When we marked a certain rock last fall the little new rosettes were hardly larger than pin-heads; now they are as large as dollars and half-dollars, but not so round and regular. The outline of a single plant is very sportive, but they all grow at a right angle from the surface to which they cling—that is, it does not make any difference to these air-plants whether they are right side up or upside down or sidewise. It seems still more out of the regular order of things to see orchids grow in the tropics from the perpendicular face of a rock, with the foliage all spread out as if it were lying on the ground, and the flower stalk extending into space perpendicularly to the rock on which it grows, of course, but horizontally to our eyes. The bees find the earliest blossoming trees, and on a springy March day one has only to stop and listen to discover which trees have opened their little brown flowers filled with honey already distilled for the busy bee.

Before this month is gone the trees will be more bare of leaves than at any time since last April. Many of the varieties of oak retain a great portion of their leaves until the swelling buds of the springtime push them off. The russet foliage does not make the prettiest kind of woods in winter, and the rattling of the dried leaves in the wind is weird and doleful. The skeletons of trees are always interesting and make beautiful tracery against the sky—the rugged oaks, the graceful elms, and the white-satiny sycamores, with here and there a dark pine showing through. Ours is mainly oak woods, and is literally brown with leaves all winter long. I have never been able to count the varieties of oak here, but there are more than we have in Kansas, and not so many as are indigenous to the Southern States. The mast, or "shack," is one of the dependable products of the region, and the animals that range for miles in the woods and feed upon it afford a home-cured ham that is as sweet and gamey as venison. Some of the local names of the oaks are very interesting and suggestive. For instance, the oak that, for some inscrutable reason, is called by the botanists the "turkey oak" is, "really," so an old colored "uncle" told me, the "turkey-track" oak. The leaf is deeply and sharply lobed, and looks not unlike a turkey-track. There are oaks that a novice could only distinguish as oaks because they bear acorns, and others that we would all recognize instantly from their likeness to the picture in the primer where "O" stood for oak, and the noble tree was thus early impressed upon our minds as the symbol of strength.

All winter the bluejays and the cardinals have flashed among the brown leaves, keeping company with the crows and the owls and the chickadees. The robins and the bluebirds came late in February, and now we have the orioles and the wrens and many more. Have you ever noticed how many of the soberly-dressed birds have especially beautiful forms— the trim little titmouse with its topknot, for one? They all have their new spring suits on now, for

"In the spring a fuller crimson comes upon the robin's
    breast;
In the spring the wanton lapwing gets himself another
    crest;
In the spring a livelier iris changes on the burnished
    dove."

Are we deceived, or do we all grow younger when the year is young?

THE CAVE AND THE MILL.

In this region of limestone rocks and running waters there are many hidden caves and many with small and obscure entrances, but our cave opens with a noble arch sixty feet in height and in beautiful proportion. A mighty keystone of nature's own chiseling supports the sides, and a series of exquisitely constructed arches, growing smaller as they recede into the hill, leads the wanderer over a rock-strewn floor, under which rumbles the buried stream. A strange, mysterious light pervades the long gallery, and you wonder whence it comes. Although the entrance is large, it does not seem as if the light could penetrate so far, and involuntarily you look up and about for an opening, or "chimney," as the miners call it. There is nothing but solid rock to be seen. Suddenly, at a turn of this underground way, you see a vista of foliage leading up a little cañon, and you realize that the cave is not a cave, but a tunnel, reaching entirely through the hill and opening again in a much smaller arch to admit the little stream

The Old Mill.

and the gentle breeze that in the hottest summer
day makes the cave delightfully cool. Both
of these outer arches are hung round with ferns
and wild columbine, clinging, stunted cedars,
five-leaved ivy, and bitter-sweet vines. Enorm-
ous rock-masses have fallen long ago from the
top and sides of the great arch, but it seems now
to have reached a section where the keystone-
mass is so perfect and the side-thrust so
evenly balanced that it may stand for ages
without further disturbance. Indeed, there is
much evidence that this great piece of nature's
architecture has existed in about its present
state for a very long time. When the Osage
Indians were the monarchs of central Missouri
this cave-tunnel was one of their strongholds.
From the top of the hill, now wooded and grass-
covered, there is a fine prospect up and down
the little stream, and a sentry stationed there
could instantly warn the warriors concealed in
the cave of the approach of friend or foe.

At the time of the Civil War, when the
people of this portion of Missouri were perhaps
as evenly divided into friends and foes of the
Government as were the people in any section
of the United States, the cave served as a
refuge, a rallying-point, and a store-house for

first one side and then the other. Here the
fugitive slave has hidden, hard pressed and
often captured; and here the renegade, the
horse-thief, and the tramp have camped and
rested for a night. But it is not for such as
these that the cave is a rendezvous to-day. It
is as a lovers' resort, a trysting-place, that now
it decks its stones with moss and scatters touch-
me-nots and buttercups along its trickling
stream. Here must come all true lovers to
plight their troth and linger in the dim lights
and indigo shadows of the cave, or their be-
trothal it not complete.

To the cave come picnickers, old and young,
for many miles about; but it is yet possible to
select a day when none but your very own will
invade the sanctuary; when you can go alone
and call it yours, and people it only with the
images of the mind.

Not far from the cave, but happily out of
sight, there is an old mill, now rapidly falling
into decay, but still telling its story of great
usefulness and importance. Both Union sol-
diers and rebels, captured and recaptured it and
manufactured supplies in it. A lumber mill, a
woolen mill, and a grist mill of no mean ca-
pacity, it was a valuable possession to either

army. Now the great water-wheel is rusted
fast on its axis; the moss-covered flume that
overshot and filled its once dripping buckets is
sagging and tottering to its fall; the floods have
burst the rotting oaken breastwork that once
held the waters back; and the wild stream goes
tumbling down its rocky way as it did before the
hand of man planted obstructions in its progress.
It no longer has the corn to grind and the fleece
to card and spin and weave, and the walnut
logs to saw into siding and flooring. Within its
walls the hoppers stand empty; the upper and
the nether mill-stones no longer grind—unless it
be to grind out memories. Yes, like the mills of
the gods, they grind slow, but they grind ex-
ceeding fine. If you sit down close beside them,
where the sunlight sifts through the lace-work
of the old clapboarded roof, you can hear them
turning, turning, slowly, invisibly, and always
backwards, to the busy days before the war and
before the blessed peace. The Civil War is still
the great milestone with all the old native hill-
people. All calculations of time, backwards or
forwards, begin at that era. I remember when
once I was in the far South to welcome a certain
soldier of the Spanish-American War, the people
told me that they were glad to have a new date

to reckon from. Their volunteers and ours
went out together to rescue Cuba from Spain,
and it made another epoch. The Spanish War
did not reach to the heart of Missouri. Hold!
I am wrong. I take it back.

We stopped to talk with a picturesque old
man of the woods one day, who said that he had
never been to either Kansas City or St. Louis—
Jefferson City having been the limit of his am-
bition, and that nearly stifled him!

"So you were born and have lived right here
all your life?" I asked.

"Oh, no!" he said. "I was borned four
mile from whar I be now; but I have been a-
cuttin' bresh on this yere farm for sixty-odd
year."

He cracked a feeble joke or two about getting married sometime because it was so lone-
some "down thar"; and said that his motto was
"While there's life there's hope." We left him
smoking his cob pipe, leaning on his grubbing
hoe, and serenely contemplating the world of
"bresh" that yet remained unconquered.

But it is never safe to jump to general con-
clusions. Before we reached home my kind-
hearted companion picked up an old man along
the way to give him a lift in our vacant seat.

Woman-like, I wished to follow the lead of our recent interesting conversation, and pretty soon said:

"Were you ever out of Morgan County?"

"Fit four year," was the laconic answer.

"Which side was he on?" He did not say: I did not ask. Both had reasons. If, however, you think that it does not make any difference in this region now-a-days you are greatly mistaken—but that is another story.

At another time I went into a country store, where all the old-time necessities were sold— corn meal and salt and tobacco and grindstones and "long-sweetening," together with such modern luxuries as barbed wire and glass lamps and patent medicines. The young man who waited upon me was so slow and lank and uncouth that I said to myself, "Here is a native of the hills that has never crossed the borders of his own State; there can be no mistake this time." So I ventured:

"Have you ever been outside of Missouri?"

"Clim San Juan Hill."

And the eye that had seemed expressionless twinkled. The patriot is everywhere, God bless our native land.

Many roads and bridle-paths converge at the

cave and the mill, and it is easy to lose the way.
Many of the tracks lead to a tie-cutter's camp, a
coal-bank, a lead or zinc mine, a potter's clay
deposit, or other small and poorly-developed
enterprise, and stop there; others "carry" you
to a cabin and a small clearing that is buried in
the woods, and still more straggle off and lose
themselves amidst the trees. The only way to
be sure of your ground, if you are a stranger, is
to ask of every tie-hauler you meet, "Is this the
way to the cave?" If you are by chance on the
right road he will tell you to "keep on the main-
plain until you come to the next notched tree on
the right, then turn off on the pale road, and
angle acrost till you come to the upper end of
the big ravine. Onct araound that, you can't
miss hit. You jest go on deown hill twell you
come to the crick, ford hit, and thar you are,
right at the cave."

The "notched" trees are wayside oaks blazed
with three nicks, each one made by two strokes
of the axe, and marking the county roads,
or, in other words, the roads that go to some
place. The notches are not placed on the side
of the tree facing the road, but on the two sides
facing the traveler as he approaches, so that he
may see them from afar.

The Cave.

The "county" road bears no relation to sectional lines in this hilly country, and after one has gone up and down, around, and over several hills, he finds that his sense of the compass has forsaken him. He must determine both time and direction by the sun. An "hour by sun" will not give him time to get home from any place; he must start at least two hours by sun, and then the chances are that he will have to depend upon the moon for the last of his journey. But it will all be charming to every sense—the eye, the ear, the soul. The mystic moonlight of the woods is like no other at any time or place. Whether it is the effulgent glow of the full-orbed lantern, as it hangs yellow and mellow in the clear sky, or the fainter glow of the sickle moon and its starry satellites, it is an enchanted world that the half-light reveals and yet conceals. Most glorious of all is it to see the gibbous moon, riding like an anchored boat on drifting clouds, black and silver, massed in great billows like the waves of the sea, tossing and tearing themselves to shreds, and yet never unmooring the tiny golden ship of the sky. One moment it is obliterated quite, in the next it swings suddenly forth into the clear space and strains at the line; then the silver edge of the cloud comes on and turns it pale, and lo! it is overwhelmed again, lost for a long minute. In such a changing light the mysticism of the woods deepens. The imagination can see all things in its depths, and there is none to say you nay.

BUTTERCUPS AND ANEMONES.

How long was the earth without form, and void?

When God had said, "Let there be light," and had set the firmament on high, and caused the waters to divide and the dry land to appear, and the grass and the herbs and the trees to grow, did that make the earth beautiful?

Until the soul of man was created and looked forth through comprehending eyes the earth was without form, and void. Before man came upon the scene there was no form, no color, no beauty, no sound. There would be none now, if his soul were not attuned to the harmony of these wondrous things. Behold, I have given you all, saith the Lord. All that the world contains is ours, for we have eyes to see, ears to hear, soul to feel. One brief lifetime affords but a glimpse, it is true; therefore, the more need of industry. We are all transcendentalists at some period of life, knowing the limits of neither time nor space—thus we live longer and travel farther. If we cannot dream in the woods,

there are Emerson and Thoreau on the book
shelves.   But do not be deceived by long asso-
ciation.   All books are as dry bones compared
with the woods in spring.   Pity the man who in
his little span has seen

"No theaters of oaks around him rise"

and watched the play therein; nor sat under

"Those green-robed Senators of the mighty woods,"

and imbibed wisdom.

Come, then, to the wildwood, if you want
inspiration to greater things, or surcease from
sorrow.

The groves of hard maple that used to
abound here have nearly all been sacrificed by
the axe, and the sugar-camp is no longer a
feature of the early spring.   A few trees are
scattered through the lowland woods, and here
and there in the open stands a noble specimen,
with its symmetrical outline and its umbrageous
shade.   I have often seen the purplish sheen of
the "Impressionists" reflected from this dense
shade and so, of course, have you.   Another
surface that in many lights gives back this irri-
descence is the gray fibre of the old fence-rails.
There are miles of "stake-and-rider" fence here,
made of rails that must have been split in Abra-

ham Lincoln's time, now covered with the loosened and weather-polished splinters of white-oak and hickory that radiate a lavender light, so brilliant sometimes that if you catch a glint of it through the squawberry and hazel bushes at the roadside as you ride by you think it is a new flower. This lovely tint appears in the valley mists on certain delicious evenings, and an artist could often find it on the rocky precipices and the log cabins. I must confess that I have never yet seen a purple cow, but that is probably because I do not look long enough at cows. I have always thought that it was a shame to obscure a landscape, even with Troyon's cows. I prefer sheep. But in the heart of Missouri there are several kinds of domestic animals in large numbers that are more picturesque than cows—mules and goats and turkeys.

There is no royalty in woods-roaming, but it does cost time and experience to acquire a woodscraft that is reliable. The mossy side of the tree is not always the north side, and where the highways bear necessarily more relation to the hills and hollows than to the section lines, the points of the compass lose themselves very often. Yes, there's the sun, but when you

cannot see it for hills and trees and clouds, and
you do not know just what time it is, nor exactly how far from home you are—well, it be-
hooves you to find the wigwam; it has evidently
gone astray, too.

Looking down the brook to-day you can
see a bright green spot, where the stream has
widened out in a marshy flat—that is *simplo-
carpus fœtidus*, one of the few things whose Latin
names I prefer to the English. Even of this
noxious plant I heard an interesting story; it
was told by Mary Rogers Miller, lecturer on
nature study at Cornell University. She was
"looking for things" one day in early February,
and came to a snow-covered bog that was dotted
over with round holes, some only large enough
for a chipmunk to slip into, and others much
larger. Peeping in, she saw this earliest and
sturdiest of green things; some plants with their
hoods yet on, and others with their uncovered
flower-stalks near the surface. The heat gen-
erated by the growing plant had melted air
holes, and about each one was a beautiful
smooth arch of snow.

A most enticing path branches off from the
brook just before the green spot is reached, and
leads up hill to Rock Spring and a little farther

Nature's Window.

on to "Aunt Fanny's" cabin. You cannot help
stopping at the spring, whether you have
brought a cup or not; and it will richly repay
you to call at the cabin. Aunt Fanny was a slave
who toiled in the hempfields of Tennessee in slavery days, and her story is as interesting as James
Lane Allen's in "The Reign of Law." But her
"life pardner" is the philosopher of the family.
His favorite topic is "women," and he not in-
frequently gives evidence of having studied his
subject pretty thoroughly in the course of his
time "befoh and endurin' the wah," as well as
since, though since that great epoch in the life
of all the old slaves his lines have fallen in far
different surroundings.

"Women is mos'ly all alike," he said to me
one time, "but when you find one 'at 's diffunt
she 's apt to be mighty diffunt. Now, thar 's
Miss Tildy; she was my ole mars's youngest
gal; jest like a picter, she was, but dat flighty
she min's you of a bird—you gwine put your
han' on hit an' hit 's done gone. I seed a sight
o' carryin' on 'mongs' quality folks in my time,
but I hain't nuver seed nobody what could
kotch up wid Miss Tildy, man nor woman—
specially no man."

"Did she never marry?" I asked.

"Oh, yes! Tuck up wid a crooked stick at las', jus' like a fool woman, when she might o' had her pick and chice of the whole of Fairfax County. She's daid now, long ago, worrited herself plum out. But the man she mout hev married—and I 'se pintedly sure she wanted to marry—is livin' yit; a big man, too. You 'd know him, I reckon, ef I 'd name him, but the secrets ob my fambly am safe in dis ole bre's'. De las' time he kim down here in de woods to talk over ole times I tole him dat de onlies' mistake he made was in not marryin' her anyhow, 'jections or no 'jections."

The old man did not get his ideas concerning the proper method of taming a shrew from Shakespeare, either.

Hanging on the cabin wall were three or four large gourds with round holes cut in them quite near the handle. When I asked to what use she put them, Aunt Fanny told me that they were her bird-houses.

"I don't hang them out in the trees twell about the time for the singin' birds to build their nestes, else the sparrows would 'propriate all of 'em." I took the valuable hint, and kept my bird-houses in until the first of April.

"That's the pizen oak," she said, pointing

to a delicate pink vine creeping up the bole of a
tree that stood near the path down which we
started. "Hit doesn't pester me, but mebbe
you all had better turn out 'n the path a ways.
Hit 's dangerous to pizenable people to go too
nigh it when the wind is blowin'. Hit 's jes' the
three-leaf that 's pizen, you know."

The first dog-tooths and buttercups and
spring-beauties and anemones blossom high up
on the hillsides, because it is warmer there than
in the bottom of the ravine, and we soon had our
hands full of tiny refreshing things.

As yet—the first week in April—they are
only open here and there, and one has to search
for them, but in a fortnight more the ground will
be besprent with pink and white and yellow
stars—no, not blue; the violets will not be out
before the first of May and not in their prime till
the middle.

I wonder if the anti-dandelion league of
Topeka has seen Miss Alice Henkel's little pam-
phlet on weeds. She was employed by the
Agricultural Department at Washington to in-
vestigate the value of plants for crude drugs.
It reveals such a curious and happy arrange-
ment. Scarcely any nutritious food-stuffs are
used in the manufacture of drugs. They are

nearly all made of weeds! Last year 115,522
pounds of dandelion weeds was imported at the
rate of from four to six cents a pound! Miss
Henkel points out the fact that European
farmers utilize many kinds of weeds that
Americans spend valuable time in trying to
exterminate.

It seems a pity, too, to class as weeds such
pretty things as

"Dandelion flowers,
All gilt with dew, as suns with showers."

When the Water is Low.

IS NATURE A SPENDTHRIFT OR A WISE ECONOMIST?

Whether Nature is a prodigal, sowing her seeds in waste places with a careless disregard of consequences, or whether she is a great economist, depends wholly upon how you view her plan. Here are millions and millions of forest tree seeds lost in a soil that is not quite adapted to their growth. Some fall upon stony places, some in the stream, and others where there is already as much vegetation as can find space and sustenance. But in the out-of-the-way corners on the broad, bare field that the fire has devastated, on the newly formed sand bar in the river, wherever there is a foothold for a tree, there also is found the seed ready to spring up. A seed is much less than a tree. "Why not, then," says Dame Nature, "provide a seed for every foot of earth that can nourish a tree."

In the Missouri orchards, where the big red apple grows, the myriads of blossoms paint a pink landscape that is wonderful to behold. To be sure, more blossoms waste their sweetness

than form apples, but the original intention of
the apple was to produce trees as well as pre-
mium fruit, and the budded trees send forth blossoms in as great profusion as the wild crab that
grows in the fence corners of these same orchards.   Never can any flower of field or garden
rival the wild crab in daintiness of form or delicacy of odor.   Its oval buds hang like drops of
ruby from every branch, and when they burst,
send forth an attar surpassing that of roses. Thus
these fair blossoms fulfill a mission upon earth,
even though few of them are perfected as fruit
and seed.

Wherever the forest-tree seeds have been sufficiently moistened to cause the germ to expand
and burst the nut or shell, there will be seen first
a little green curl at one end, apparently uncer-
tain which way to grow and what form to take.
But in reality there is no uncertainty whatever
in this tiny forerunner of a great tree.   The form
less first shoot is the root, feeling its way to the
earth, in which it will take hold and thus fasten
for life a tree in that particular spot, provided all
the conditions sustain the effort of the seedling.

It is evident that if millions of seeds were not
provided, there would be no certainty that one
at least would fall upon every favored spot.

When we get down to the bottom of things we
find that Nature, lavish as she is, is yet always
provident.

The wild-flower gardens have been quick to
respond to the rare opportunity of this backward
season. The cold weather has retarded the
growth of the tree foliage, and thus more light
and air and sunshine have been afforded the
wild-flowers. A little cool weather does not
daunt them, and they have thrived this spring
in great luxuriance and beauty. Just now, the
north-side rocks are hung with columbine.
Doesn't it make you think of Tennyson, and
"airy, fairy, Lillian"? So graceful and so light
is the swaying blossom. Three shades of the
wild phlox besprinkle the upland woods floor
now, and wherever loamy banks have formed by
the wash of multitudinous rains along the foot of
the hills, blue bells are ringing their fairy chimes,
and sending an answering note of color to the
sky. A little higher up the "blue-eyed grass"
appears, for shy as it is, this country is yet
enough of a wilderness to cherish it. It blooms
right in among the white star grass, but quite dis-
tinct from it. Still another blue flower of the late
spring-time is the wild larkspur, dark and rich,
almost purplish in hue, seeking the moist corners

and the varying shade.   The waxy blossom of
the may-apple is budding now under the broad
web-footed leaf, the little umbrellas of the woods.

"Perhaps the best thing anyone who has seen
a Missouri hillside thickly covered with anemones and phlox growing together can do, is to
turn away and see nothing more for that day, so
as to carry away a perfect memory of delicate
delight."   I wish that I had said that myself, but
you shall have the benefit of it though Fielding
Lewis uttered it.

Did you ever observe the phosphorescent
light of flowers?   There is a little orange-yellow
blossom in the woods now, profusely scattered
amongst all the other varieties, much like the
English primrose in form, that emits a faint light
in the evening and early twilight, as many bright
yellow flowers do.   It was a woman, the daugh-
ter of the famous botanist, Linnæus, who first
saw, or at least first recorded her observation of
the light radiating from a bunch of nasturtiums.
Yellow is the most luminous of colors and many
yellow flowers, including our own sunflower, and
the California poppy, have been seen to emit this
inexplicable glow.

"The May," as our English cousins call the
hawthorn bloom, is now in its prime, and the
little trees are as picturesque as the Japanese

picture trees. Gnarled like a great oak, tough as hickory and every twig spined with a score of sharp points, it is fruitless labor to try to secure a bough to carry home unless armed with a hatchet. It is foolish to go to the woods at any time without a hatchet and a knife and a trowel and basket—and a luncheon. The joy of God's outdoors cannot be realized in an hour. One must penetrate the thickets, and sit by the talking brook, and wander where the breeze whispers low—all shut in by trees. Listen to the mocking bird! He is ringing his rhapsody from the tree top, ever vying with, and ever outdoing his relatives, the catbird and the brown-thrasher. He is a social bird, building his nest low, only ten or twelve feet from the ground usually, and near to the primitive hill-cabins and in the orchards. He is brave, too, never hesitating to attack an animal that ventures too near his chosen bough, and fearless of man as well. Perhaps he knows that his song will protect him.

The black philosopher of the hills agrees with a certain weather prophet of Kansas. He says we shall have a wet spring and a dry summer, and we know that they are both at least half right. It would seem that even the Kansas wheat fields must be moistened all over by this time, and in Missouri every hill-stream is run-

ning like a mountain torrent, so that the woods-
people cannot come to the village until the water
runs down.   In the length and breadth of this
old county there is not a bridge over one of the
many creeks, and if bridges were built I think it
would necessitate a law, such as there is in certain districts of Mexico, to compel the people to
drive over them.   Such a pleasure it is to go
splashing through the clear, pebbly-bottomed
brooks!   The horses like it as well as the people,
and drink at every opportunity.   The little
ponies that are bought out in the hills and
brought to town to wear their lives away as liv-
ery teams for prospective investors, often nearly
perish of thirst before they will drink of the min-
eral-impregnated water of the deep bored well.
The driver who does not unrein his horse when
he is to cross a stream or climb a steep hill is
inhuman, and certainly must answer for his
cruelty in some way.   Many of the water courses
in Missouri have French names, as our nearby
beautiful creek, the Gravois, and the Gasconade
River, which is the ideal fishing ground for St.
Louisians.

Every State contiguous to Missouri must
have a town named Versailles, I think. The
French emigrants who went out from old St.
Louis to found new settlements in the wilderness,

Columbine Ledge.

were loyal to their motherland and chose the
name of the capital of France in many instances.
The Spaniards left their mark on the nomencla-
ture of the State also, and hard-by we have Moro
Creek. A little farther away runs the Indian
Osage, a river that is navigable for many miles
southwest of Jefferson City, near which place it
empties into the Missouri. So much of the history of a country can be best preserved in the
names of localities and natural features that it
is a matter of serious importance to fix a name
upon a lake or a river, a mountain or a town.
Wherever the poetical Spaniards tarried they
chose some lovely hilltop and dedicated it to the
blessing of good health, calling it Montesano,
a foreign term that anyone with the slightest
knowledge of root words may translate. Perhaps this pretty custom caused the citizens of
a portion of Arkansas to petition to be taken
into the confines of the commonwealth of Missouri. You know that the maps of Missouri and
Arkansas show a little foot or offset, to have
been taken off the upper corner of Arkansas,
along the Mississippi River, and added to the
lower eastern corner of Missouri. That was a
very "sickly" region at one time, and the
natives succeeded in having it transferred for
that reason into a more "healthy" State.

MAY-DAY.

"I, country born and bred, know where to find
  Some blooms that make the season suit the mind
  An' seem to match the doubtin' bluebird's notes.

"Half-venturin' liverworts in furry coats,
  Bloodroots, whose rolled-up leaves if you uncurl,
  Each on 'm's cradle to a lovely pearl.

"But these ur jes' spring's freaks, sure ez sin
  The rebel frosts 'll try to drive 'em in,
  For half our Mays so awfully like Maynt,
    'Twould rile a Shaker or a average saint.

"Though I own up I like our back'ard springs
  That kind o' tozzle with their greens and things;
  An' when you 've most give up, without more words,
  Toss the fields full o' blossoms, leaves, an' birds.

"That 's northern natur', slow, an' apt to doubt.
  But when it does git stirred—there 's no gin out."

In spite of the lingering winter the last week
of April saw the woods full of redbud and dogwood and serviceberry blossoms, and the beautiful sand-violet is blooming in greater luxuriance than ever. It should more appropriately

be called the gravel-violet, for to secure the
roots one has to insert a knife-blade between
the tightly-packed stones of the hillside and
force the plant out. The local name for this
peculiar variety of the violet is the "wild
pansy." The reason for this is that the two
upper petals are velvety, like a pansy petal.
Or, you may call it the larkspur-violet, if you
like, because of the resemblance of the leaves, or
the *violetta delphinfolia*, which is very pretty.
It is like the common blue violet in being stem-
less, both the leaf and the flower-stalk springing
directly from the root. The yellow and the
white branching violet grow here in profusion a
little later, and the violet with the "bird's-foot"
leaf, so common on the Eastern mountains, is
found here, but the loveliest varieties are the
dear old blue flower with the heart-shaped leaf
that grows in every State in the Union, and the
velvety-petaled, tri-colored beauty with the almost fern-like leaf. The real johnny-jump-up
lives in the stony nooks and shady corners here,
too; its blossoms not larger than a grain of corn,
and its slender branching stem creeping along
close to the ground! What a contrast there is
between its small pale face and those of its
royal-purple sisters in the garden! I know of

no flower that shows the triumph of cultivation more pleasingly.   No doubt all of the ten va- rieties set down by the botanists as belonging to the country west of the Mississippi are to be found here, but some are more shy than others. It is the enchanting blue carpet of the velvety ones, spread first on the southern slopes and then on the northern, that is worth coming to see.

In the last two weeks the bluejays have al- most disappeared, and I miss their flashing flights, their noisy squawk, and their sweet call that we are so rarely privileged to hear from a far treetop.   They had a great jubilee in the trees about our house one day, flying round and round and back and forth in a flock for several hours; then they separated into pairs and went their way for the summer, many of them farther north.   Their cousins the crows remained with us, but they held the same kind of a jollification amongst themselves when the winter flock broke up into individual families.

I have listened this spring for the song of the bobolink, hoping that the Ozark hills might at- tract him, and because Professor Goss says that there is a specimen in the Kansas State House that he shot in May, 1877, near Neosho Falls, thus proving that this greatest of American singers has been in the West; but I have not heard him, and my New England friends in Topeka, who are naturally always listening for bob olinks in the spring, say that they have never heard one in Kansas. So I conclude that Pro fessor Goss is right when he says that " the bobo link is rare and 'exceptional in the West."

The great swelling buds of the hickory, all swathed in pink satin, are bursting now, and the little green hands are reaching forth into the balmy air. The silvery-gray catkins are waving and the willow twigs are shining in their yellow-green armor, like a myriad of tiny lances in the sun.

There are two ways to distinguish black oak and white oak. The bark of the black oak is blackish and the bark of the white oak is whitish. If you look through the forest with this distinction in mind, even if you are a woman, you can see the difference. When the leaves begin to come out there is another difference. The black oak leaves, in little many-pointed clusters of pinkish white, look like flowers on the end of every twig and branch. The white oak leaves are pure green without any shading, and they develop to their full size so thin and delicate that a tree hung with new leaves looks as if it were dressed with tissue paper. As the season advances the leaves thicken, and by the time autumn comes they are almost as thick and tough as the black oak leaves. The latter is the typical oak leaf of art and tradition, the one we conventionalize and use oftenest for decoration, though the white oak and the jack oak are not barred out.

Why do we not have a national flower or tree or plant? With such a variety to choose from, a choice is difficult, to be sure; but to adopt a flower emblem is a duty we owe to posterity. I do not favor the sunflower, it is neither sweet nor—as yet—useful. It has one advantage—it can be conventionalized; that the goldenrod cannot be is a serious artistic objection to it. The oak tree and the Indian corn both have good points. We are not modest enough for the violet, we cannot take the rose of England, nor the lily of France, nor the chrysanthemum of Japan—what, then, are we to do? I wish we might get together on the subject.

Coming up the ravine to-day I found the old black philosopher of the hillside modeling a scare-crow in his "goober" patch. Out of a few rags and tatters, including a flapping Missouri

A Mossy Bank.

hat with calico-lined brim, he had attitudinized a pretty fair native of the hills. The figure stood with outstretched arms, pointing a stick that looked very like a gun straight at the well-kept corner of the garden where the "goobers" were planted. The next best corner was where the " 'baccy" grows, and in between were onions and cabbages and other things less vital to existence than "goobers" and "'baccy." Everybody in Missouri fences the garden in and gives the fowls free range. This garden was enclosed, as many are, with hand-split white oak pickets about five feet high and covered with splinters, making it practically boy-tight as well as chicken-tight. "This is the old woman's yarb corner," Uncle said, turning to a clump of tansy and old-man and cardamin. "They is mighty sweet," giving the whole group a gentle stirring up with his hard hand. The air was filled with the blended aromatic odors, almost intoxicating in their fervor.

"Al'ays 'minds me of ole Mars'," continued the sage. "His favorite was boneset an' hit 's run out; but he sure did love all kinds of powerful scents. Fact is, he was a reg'lar Ratican 'mongst men—and women, too, matter o' that. You know they is one once in awhile that towers away up head an' shoulders 'bove the rest. Now, most men is like this grass, some a little taller and some a little shorter, but mostly all 'bout the same. That 's what makes a Ratican stand out so plain. He has powers that other men don't have. I heerd a preacher preach onct who told 'bout the wise men in some faraway country. He said they could lay down on the ground an' gaze at the stars twell they brung 'em down. I reckon ole Mars could, ef he had looked long enough.''

The hollyhocks had originally been planted inside the garden, but they now crowded the old picket fence on both sides, making a picture in themselves, though no flower-stalks were yet visible. The leaf in its early perfection resembles the classic acanthus, and groups itself about any nearby object in the most graceful manner. What a treasure-house an old garden is, and what a blessing and a boon to family life, in town or out! I was so glad to find a corroboration of my own views on the destruction of the private yard and garden by the modern parking system of home lots. This writer says:

"The passing of the fence is a very serious thing, and it is no wonder that our public-spirited citizens are carefully pondering over the

matter.   Privacy is the most precious jewel of
home life, says one, and no greater calamity
could befall our national character than to become indifferent to it.   The absence of it makes
for conformity in all we do, whereas its presence
encourages individual action.   It makes one
fond of home, and gives a spirit of ownership.
Seek as one will in rural America for small
houses with secluded and enclosed surroundings,
where some of the blessings of open air may be
enjoyed with a due amount of retirement, and
alas! they are not often to be found.   Everywhere the fence is despised and has been de-
stroyed."

The cloud-curtains have rolled away.   The
robin redbreast sits right in front of my window
singing his insistent evening song.   The rays of
the sinking sun strike straightly on his breast,
reminding one of the pretty Irish legend which
relates that the robin, being nearer and dearer
to the human family than any other bird, was
the first to alight on the cross after the cruci-
fixion and there received the drop of blood that
ever after tinged the feathers on its bosom.

All the signs point to fair weather once more.
The thermometer and the barometer are going
up together, and the birds fly high.   If the
signs hold we shall go a-Maying.

THE RAIN IN THE WOODS.

The world is baptized anew! Every dripping leaf shines with re-created vigor and joyousness, all the little dry ravines of yesterday are filled with the sound of laughing waters, the common stones along the brookside are washed till they glisten like cut agates, and the moss beds are greening up! What a wondrous tranformation comes in the wake of a shower. The parched earth drinks and drinks, but there is always enough left in this country of steep water-sheds to fill the little stream beds and replenish the fishing holes.

The raindrops break the surface of the water and hide the fishermen from the fish, they say, so that it is a good time to fish—if you like fishing—and I know people who will stand by the hour and look too wet and woe-begone for any use, and think they are enjoying themselves. Once upon a time we sojourned on the Florida coast, where Spanish mackerel were not only fished for, but caught and cooked inside of fifteen minutes, so the chef said, though I en-

tertained a strong suspicion that he had some
reserves on the broilers to deceive amateur
fisher folk—it is so easy to deceive people who
think it is fun to fish. They may hold a pole
for half a day without getting so much as a
nibble, then let them but catch the hook on the
root of a tree and they become so animated you
would think they had discovered a zinc mine.

However, when they do actually catch Missouri hill-stream fishes and cook them over the
coals with a little bacon in the picnic frying pan
they are far sweeter than Spanish mackerel.
The proof of the pudding is in the eating—I
have tasted both.

· How like a cushion the woods-earth is after a
rain, and how many pretty green things spring
into view that were lost in the general dryness of
a few days ago! And now, after a beginning,
how easily it rains! You see blue sky through
the treetops, quite enough to make an apron,
and you think of the old saying and decide to
continue your ramble, but immediately, quietly,
without any warning, down comes the rain
again, straight to the earth; falling softly at
first and then in a regularly ascending crescendo
till the forest vibrates with the deluge. We
think of the long twilight hours when we sat on

the high veranda and watched the majestic
clouds that rolled up over the edge of the world
and promised rain in the dry time. Great
thunder-heads, filled with forked lightning, and
tinted like the golden fleece by the sunset after-
glow. How magnificent they were, but how
empty! The flowers and the flocks alike plead
in vain; not a drop fell. There are people, men
and women, whom we all know, whose prom-
ises melt away like the rosy evening cloud and
the dry-weather lightning, without fulfillment,
leaving only disappointment as the afterpiece to
their brilliant play.

The leaves drooped under the heavy down-
pour, and even the largest trees were no protec-
tion. At the first lull we skurried back to old
black Auntie's cabin and were glad to take
refuge under its hospitable eaves.

The enveloping pipe-smoke was dry and
warm, and made a most artistic atmosphere for
the little dark interior. Winter and summer,
except on the very stormiest days, the door
stands ajar to admit light, for there is no window, and the thrifty old couple keep the spaces
between the logs well "chinked and daubed"
with chips and clay, and there were thus few
loop-holes for daylight to sift through. Over-

head hung branches of sweet herbs already
drying, those for "ailments" of both man and
beast and those for spicing the Christmas cakes.
Red peppers were strung in festoons from rafter
to rafter, and a few choice ears of early corn depended by a string out of reach of the mice from
the apex of the clapboarded roof. The gourds
that later would dry on the walls were yet
ripening outside the door on a rude rustic trellis
that black Uncle had made to please his thrifty
better-half. The three "split" bottomed chairs
had come from "ole Kaintuck" when young
Mars George "emigranted" through, but the
"splits" had been renewed with Missouri hickory about fifty years ago. The bed is the great
pride of the cabin always, and in this instance
was literally a monument of feathers and patchwork quilts. Our wet garments were hung on
the posts and over the foot-board, but none was
permitted to touch the "star of Bethlehem"
quilt that shone in white and red brilliance over
all the cushiony expanse. The old black man
and woman were both at home, and I recognized
the opportunity I had long looked for to hear
them talk about slavery times. I had asked the
old philosopher once if he could remember
hearing any of the old slaves tell of the bringing
of African negroes to this country.

"One," he said, "one old, old black mammy
my great-grand-mammy I reckon she was."

"Now," I said, as soon as we were seated
about the blaze he had started in the old stone
fireplace to "dry us out," "now, Uncle, tell us
about your great-grand-mammy."

"Well, chilluns," he began, "hit 's a big sure
'nuff turrible tale 'bout de slave ships. You
all's heerd it many a time, I reckon, but I 'se
heerd it by word o' mouf. When de ole
mammy dat I rickoleck set a-croonin' by de
chimbley an' begun to rock back an' fo'th wid
her eyes turned inwards, my mammy would say,
'She's gwine to tell 'bout de ship!' an' we all
come close to listen."

" 'Dar it comes! Dar it comes!' she would
say, 'a-sailin' an' sailin' over de sea, de sails a-
shinin' an' a puffin' out like a swan's bres', but
we all know'd what 'twas comin', for an' hit
look to us like a 'gator in de swamp. All de
people run into de woods, but we couldn't run
fas' enough. De chilluns couldn't keep up; de
mammies wid a baby under each arm give out
an' fell down in de bresch an' was cotch dar by de
men what cum frum de ship in little boats. De
black men cum back frum de woods to holp de
wimmen an' de chillun an' git cotch, too."

Old Uncle was a Louisiana negro, and used a dialect as unique as it was rich. I should make a grand failure were I to try to repeat a long story in his words. I must stick to my own, though his would be more worth the reading.

He said that the big slavers cruised along the shore for many miles, men from the little landing-boats making forays wherever they saw settlements or knew of villages. When the hunters had captured all they could of men, women, and children without endangering themselves to ambush by the natives, they took their victims to the ship's hold in relays, if it were near by; but if the boats had gone a long distance and captured many negroes they chained the men and women to trees and the children in bunches and left them, sometimes all night, hidden in the reeds or bushes. When the boats returned to pick up their prey some were dead, some had escaped, and others were overlooked and left to starve, if not found and rescued by the tribe after the slave-ship had disappeared.

The old mammy who told these tales had been captured as a child, and after lying all night in terror of death in a thousand forms was taken aboard the ship by sailors who came a second time to search for her because she was strong

and well formed and promised a large price.
When they looked for her the first time, in the
early morning, she lay very still among the
reeds, scarcely breathing for fear they would find
her, but by the time they came again she was
starving and afraid of the crocodile in the la-
goon, and she cried out. Of the long weeks
of the passage to America in the ship's hold
she had but a dim remembrance. She only
knew that it was horrible, endless. Many died
and all sickened. She never saw the ocean from
the time she was driven aboard until she was
carried off more dead than alive. Men and
women were walking skeletons; babies wailed in
a voice so weak and low they were hardly heard
by their mothers who bore them on their gaunt
arms. America was heaven, because it was
land—it did not rock and heave. They had air
to breathe once more and food, though it was
not what they called food in Africa and longed
for here. The ship landed at St. Augustine, and
the girl, who was fifteen years of age when she
came to the New World a captive slave, was sold
in the public market of that historic town. Because of her aptness at learning she was trained
as a house-servant, and lived for years in Florida
until she was the mother of five children. Then

she was sold to a Louisiana trader, because, her
mistress said, she was getting too "biggity."
She thought she had known as a child what the
torture of homesickness was, but when she was
put to work in the rice swamps of Louisiana,
with an overseer watching her every movement,
her heart straining like a leashed hound against
the hopelessness of it all, the memory of the ship
became as nothing. Long before this she had
learned to be a slave. She did not expect
relief or escape, even by death, and she lived to
realize the blessing of the overseer's lash that
drove her to toil, even unto sleep.

In time, other children came to her arms,
and the third era of her existence was begun.
One of these children was the mother of the old
philosopher before us, our entertainer. She was
lighter colored than he, he said, and lighter
than her mother, for the gradations of com-
plexion in the Afro-American race do not follow exactly according to the admixture of
blood. She was a most remarkable woman,
he remembered, though he was sold away from
her when he was a very young man. She was a
prophet and a saint, and could work such
wonders on her fellow-slaves, her lovers, and her

master, that some said she was a "blue-gum," but that was not true.

When "ole Mars" emigrated north to Kentucky he took the story-teller, then almost grown to manhood, along, and he was the only comfort of his mother, for all the rest of her second set of children were left behind in Louisiana. In less than a year he was sold to a slave-trader and taken down the Mississippi in a chain-gang of high-priced men. He never saw his mammy again, but the fortunes of his race brought him back to Kentucky.

"That gran' ole State, nor Missouri nuther," he said, "don't know much about the slave times we all knowed in Louisiana. Ole Mars, was mighty good to us all. That's whar me an' Fanny met up wid one nuther, an' we hain't nuver been pahted. We all loss a powerful lot when de wah ruin de ole plantation, an' we hatter pull up stakes agin an' come on to Missouri."

"Would you like to go back to Kentucky and the plantation and be taken taken care of by a kind master again?" I asked.

"No, no, Miss, I kain't say dat; I kain't say dat in truf."

And I never have found one ex-slave that

would, though many of them are very proud of their "white folks."

The rain was over, and it was time to go home before the old black man had touched upon the tales in minor chords, of which he knows so many concerning slavery time.

AUTUMN IN THE WOODS.

If ever the artist has sojourned in this picturesque region I do not know, but he might
well do so: there is material worth while.
Looking out over the waves of color to-day, I
wondered if it were not about time for the
modern painters to give us autumn studies
again. You know it has been the fashion ever
since the impressionists appeared in this country
to portray springtime landscapes almost ex-
clusively. The enticing greens with the purple
lights shimmering on them—they have become
lovely to us all, whether we would or not. But
why abandon wholly the autumnal glories?
For one, I long to see them from the new school
view-point. There is no reason why they
should not be natural. But fashion in art
changes unaccountably, like fashion in everything else. It is the only thing that ever takes
place without a traceable reason, yet, in common with everything else, fashions have their
cycles; for that reason, if for no other, we shall
again have the autumn scene, and the artist of

to-day, like those great woods interpreters, Co-
rot and Inness, will spread before us the story of
the year from earliest springtime to the fall of
the leaf.

Just now, a night and a day make visible
changes in the woodland tints. The russets and
the bronzes spread and grow deeper at the same
time; the beautiful yellows appear to supply the
high-lights to the picture and the deep reds to
give it tone and richness.

There is a great deal of beautiful country between Topeka, Kansas, and the heart of Missouri. One of the prettiest bits of it lies along
the Kaw Valley. An almost imperceptible sug-
gestion of autumn was creeping into the foliage
of the hillsides, but they still wore a richer
summer green than any other hills I saw.

My favorite seat is always on the side next
to the hills when coming down to Kansas City,
but this time I was attracted to the other side
by the Kaw Valley potato-diggers. They were
at work by the scores for many miles along the
way, and they immediately suggested Millet's
famous picture of the peasant potato-diggers of
France—but only by contrast. The peasant's
blouse and his wooden shoes are more picturesque than the garb of the Kansas farmer,

but his stolid face tells a story that cannot be read in Kansas.   In the alert eye of the Kansas potato-digger one can see prefigured both the cost and the outcome of the crop, and he smiles and whistles, and plans his new barn and the addition to his house.   No man can foretell to what estate he may achieve.   The peasant will simply dig potatoes to the end of his days.

Beyond Kansas City the country presented a blue and gold edition of nature from morning till night.   The fields were flaming with goldenrod, and blackeyed Susans marched in solid ranks along the highways and byways.   Here and there might be seen a dash of purple, but autumn's own color, yellow, in all its lovely tints and shades, prevailed.   The color that railroad men say can be seen farther than any other, and that artists call an "advancing" color, for the same reason, really lighted up the entire country on this day, and the blue, blue sky was over all.

In this setting were many beautiful pictures. One was composed of a ploughed and harrowed field that lay ready for the fall sowing.   It was as smooth and fine as if those expert gardeners of Kansas, D. W. Wilder, of Hiawatha, and J. K. Hudson, of Topeka, had digged it with their

On the Moro.

own hands. Next it was a field of partly
ripened corn, bordered along the edge with a
fruitful pumpkin vine, and, beyond that, a ridge
covered with the big-leaved scrub oak, just
giving a hint of its October hues. The scale of
colors was perfect, and the picture was not im-
pressionistic, but late in the afternoon I saw one
that was. We ran into a Missouri River sand-
flat that was studded with the white boles of
dead sycamore trees. They were gaunt and
ghostly looking, long since denuded of all but
the stumps of their limbs, and presenting none
of the fine tracery of a perfect tree skeleton.
The nakedness of one was clothed, to be sure,
in a clinging vine-robe, all the leaves deftly
shingled one above another to the very top.
But it only served to emphasize the forlornness
of the others. The water-gullied banks that led
up to higher ground were set with " snow-on-the-
mountain," whose whitish-green "washed" into
the background beautifully. The only scraps of
color in the picture were furnished by the vine
and a group of barefoot little girls in faded pink
calico gowns who played in the gray sand. As
a piece of realism, it was ugly and dreary, but it
would be beautiful as a water-color, treated in a
"broad" style, and it reminded me of a picture

that youthful fancy long ago hung in my private gallery. You will all remember it—it is the tapestry that hangs over Mr. Somebody's door in "Middlemarch." George Eliot said that it "represented a blue-green world with a pale stag in it."

A great argument for the impressionists is the fact that we mortals only open our eyes wide enough to see the high-lights of life, and thus miss all the fine finish and detail of things. The devotees of impressionism believe that around the "focus," wherever that point is located in a picture, details may be worked out with some approach to precision—"insistence," I believe they call it—and that radiating from this point everything must become less and less insistent, more and more formless, until those portions of the canvas farthest removed from the focus shall become void, though they must be still harmonious. There is logic in this theory, because a landscape painting is nature condensed. In nature the eye cannot carry to the farther side of a meadow and distinguish the leaves on a tree, nor to the remotest sheep in a flock and see the woolly texture of its fleece. We have to make allowance for distance and to remember that in a degree a picture is all distance. But before the eye can comprehend the grand harmonies of either nature or art it must have observed the delicacy and completeness of detail in the original. There is but one book and one teacher for this lesson. The pages of the book are spread upon the face of the earth, and the teacher is the heart that looks through the eye of man.

In our first ramble in the autumn woods we had the good fortune to be lost. Up hill and down dale for miles and miles, without much regard to roads, is apt to lose the points of the compass for any who are not wise in woodscraft. We were led on and on by the wonderful glow, almost flame-like it was. A low-growing bush with a small maple-shaped leaf spread like fire over the ground, and overhead the tracery of gold was drawn upon the sky. The like of that spot I have never seen in any other part of the world. It was an enchanted land, worth going many miles to see, and yet we travel all around these wild hills seeking for beauty-spots. The woods thickened and cedars sprang up out of the flames, grew closer and closer together until we could hardly make our way through them, and the cushion of needles under our feet grew softer and deeper. Then, a gentle light began to filter

through the trees in front of us, and we knew
that we were on the brink of an "opening."
Parting the low-growing branches and stepping
out, we found ourselves on the grassy bank of
a little valley.   Long blades of blue grass lay
like a rich drapery over the incline, and we
stopped to rest on its cool, moist surface.   What
is a landscape without it!   The world's richest
zone is girdled by grass.   On one side of it lies
the land of snows, on the other stretch the ever-
lasting sands.   The snows may be illumined by
the resplendent lights of the aurora borealis, and
the sands may be diapered with the many-hued
flowers of the tropics, but lacking the softening
touch of grass, the picture also lacks finish.

Looking across the valley from our emerald
couch we saw a wall of woods hung with the
rich tapestries of autumn.   A great splash of
red and purple blended was made by the foliage
of the wild cherry, and a band of yellow ran
half way round the crescent of the valley and
shaded off into a faded elm.   Once in a while
there is a sportive elm that takes on a beautiful
yellow, but oftener the elm leaves simply fade
out, and when the division cells between leaf
and twig let go they flutter down to earth un-
noticed.   Below the golden band of color there

was a willow grove, yet green and fresh-looking, making a close cover for many families of small woods creatures. On the other side of the valley every tree wore a royal robe of different hue, and that vague, sad questioning that comes with the autumn atmosphere said: "Why must it all disappear so soon?" Perhaps it is like the glory of a sunset, or the sound of a great chord—too magnificent to last, too tense for the eye, the ear, the soul.

Truly this is the "fifth season," this Indian Summer of the temperate zone. There is nothing comparable to the veiling, violet mists of morning, the rosy haze of twilight, the languorous spell. But here comes the warning West Wind in a little gust that scatters a many-colored shower of leaves. No more the sighing south breeze—that gentle fan of summertime that moves mysteriously through the woods. Look upon the pageant of color quickly before it is too late. The margin of the brook that ran through the valley was the favorite haunt of the gentian, a shy flower, though decked in the bluest blue under the sky. Down to this border-land of earth and heaven we wended our way, and soon came upon the bright blossoms shining like stars in their setting of green. Some have

their feet fairly in the water, others had set up a
colony quite out in the glade, and still others
climbed the steep hillside several yards. For
its pretty name the flower goes away back to
Gentius, a king of Illyria, who, it is said, discovered its medicinal virtues. What these are
in the pharmacopœia I do not know, but I
should put them down as "pleasing to the eye"
and "stimulating to the soul." It is hard to
find the beautiful fringed gentian, but the blue
is just as blue in the closed and partly open
varieties.

There is a legend of a slight to a fairy queen
who was denied shelter within the petals of the
gentian because of the lateness of the hour in
returning from her nocturnal flirtations. Her
ladyship avenged the slight by commanding the
petals of the prudish flower to be forever closed
to the sunlight; granting full favors, however,
to her less prudish sister as a reward for her
open hospitality.

In the genealogy of flowers the gentian ranks
high, for it is recorded by the botanists that of
the 450 species of *gentianaceæ* scattered over the
face of the earth, in barren and wet places, and
on Alpine heights, not a single one contains
poisonous properites.

We gathered a big bouquet of the beauties'
but carefully left the roots in their chosen hab-
itat. A woodsman of the region up and down
the little Meramec, near St. Louis, told me that
many varieties of wild flowers had been entirely
annihilated there by the habit of sending the
whole plant away in tiny boxes to admiring
friends. Lowell says of something else that it
"made in good sooth, like the fringed gentian, a
late autumn spring." So it will if you gather it
in our valley. Would that I might guide all
whom I love to this spot!

THE SKELETON WOODS.

And yet it is beautiful! The giant elbows of the oaks, the gracefully curving branches of the elms, the symmetrical sugar maple, the long white limbs of the leaning sycamore, the golden willow wands gleaming in the sun, and here and there an emerald cedar set like a gem in its native matrix, a cleft-rock on the hillside.

Except in some sequestered nook, the color is all gone, and one wishes that the dead brown leaves would all blow away, too. They no longer decorate the skeleton trees nor clothe them with beauty, and their constant rustling makes doleful music for the woods traveler. But the topmost branches of nearly all the trees are bare, and whether etched against a gray November sky, or on the soft haze of an Indian summer day, betray many lines of beauty in their marvelous fretwork.

The prairie fields that skirt the woods hereabout are dotted with the bunchy, prickly crab-apple tree and the umbrella-like growth of the hawthorn. Neither the black nor the red haw

tree is quite as flat-topped as the English hawthorn, but it has that picturesque habit, and is a
joy to the landscape in springtime.

I have a companion in my visits to the
skeleton woods just now who is the happy pos-
sessor of a youthful and vivid imagination, and
can thereby see, with the added aid of the full
moon, the old English abbey of Glastonbury,
set in the midst of what she has named the hawthorn field, and I think she more than half
believes that on Christmas eve a pair of woodland lovers will steal out into this *demesne* to see
the blossoms burst forth in their miraculous
whiteness. Truly it would be a beautiful sight
if this old legend of Christmas and the flowering
hawthorn could come true in Missouri.

The hickory and the walnut trees are raining
nuts this year. Every morning they come rattling down on the dry leaves in showers, and
there are scurrying squirrels and groundlings
gathering and storing them—where, no man
knoweth, unless he remember that he was once a
boy. The large nut that is known here as the
"river hickory" is sweeter and meatier than the
shellbark. It grows on the benches along the
Osage River in great luxuriance. The little
persimmon grove appropriates a space all to

itself, and the wabbly-stemmed trees stand like an awkward squad, all with crooked legs. The persimmon has been sweetened by the frost and now offers its luscious preserve to all passers— provided they have a sufficiently long pole. The pawpaw, too, hangs its banana-like fruit in tempting reach, and every once in a while we see an unmatched team and an old covered wagon, bursting with little towheads and trailing a cow or two behind, come wending its way back into the Missouri woods (even from Kansas), all because "pawpaws is ripe."

There is a great deal of both black locust and honey locust scattered through the woods here, distinctly different in form and habit, but both picturesque, and there is buckeye and dogwood and redbud and barberry and hazel amongst the lower growths. If nature leaves any waste spaces it is for a good reason.

There is one roadside bush that I wish might be utilized in Kansas as it is in a German community in central Missouri—it is the squaw-berry, or the buckberry, as you prefer to give it the Indian masculine or feminine. The people in a neighborhood of considerable size make baskets, and very pretty ones, of the tough, pliant withe of the squawberry bush, and they

The Skeleton Woods.

say that it is better than the willow, finer and
more durable. It seems too bad to permit anything to go to waste that grows in such profusion and without care. You know how we are
always tempted to gather a bunch of the berries every fall because they have such a clear
crimson color in the sun, and how disappointing
they are when we take them in the house. This
year they are perhaps no more brilliant than
usual, but they are full of berries, some of the
racemes being a quarter of a yard long and very
heavy, so that they bend gracefully, and are
really pretty against a light background. I
said the color was all gone, but we found a little
hillside field that had been grubbed for a tobacco patch, in which the young oak shoots,
thrown up late from the old roots, were bril-
liantly red. The thick waxy leaves shone like
Japanese enamel, and I thought of the woods-
woman who said that her zinnias "were 'most
as pretty as artificials."

Many times during this drive my companions
and I spoke of it as the last of the year, for soon
the snow will come, and then we will gather
about the fireplace instead of going to the
woods. There is not a "naturalist," nor a "ge-
ologist," nor a "botanist," nor a "prospector,"

nor a "capitalist" amongst us, so we do not
have to go woodsing in cold weather. When
there is just a sparkle of frost in the air, as to-
day, oh, that is delightful! And when the fire is
lighted and the blue smoke curls up into the
tree tops, and the sweet potatoes are roasting in
the coals, and the coffee simmering on the hot
stone, and the fish frying in the pan, then pre-
pare ye for a feast fit to set before the gods.
That famous old sauce, hunger, whose equal has
never been found for any viands in any land,
will season it all to your most fastidious taste,
and you will be glad that you came to the Missouri woods. Would that I could guide all woods
lovers, to the nooks and crannies that I know in
the heart of Missouri! But they must go their
way, most of them, seeking beauty afar off. The
only way to bring many people to these obscure
woods would be to pass a law like unto the old
unwritten rule of many Pennsylvania Quakers.
They held it to be an extravagance to go farther
from home than five dollars would carry them.
Now we fly in the night time over this picturesque region of central southern Missouri as if
our very lives depended upon reaching either
Kansas City or St. Louis, as the case may de-
mand. Nevertheless, here beauty-spots abound,
and some day we will find them out.

You would have been convinced that the color was not all gone if you had seen our carriage when we reached home—it was loaded with cedar boughs and bitter-sweet vines and the belated oak leaves.

Just as we drove into our own avenue of leafless locusts the sun dropped over the line from Missouri into Kansas and painted for us one of the most magnificent blue and gold sunsets that ever mortal eyes looked upon. There was not another note of color except the soft luminous grays that shaded the two tones into each other. Far down the wooded valley the mists were rising, and on the bosom of every billow was the reflection of the great overhanging canopy of blue and gold.

THE OCTOPUS OF 'POSSUM HOLLOW.

Poor old Ephram stood amongst a group of dejected-looking black people that surrounded the monster—a steam wood-sawing machine—that had invaded the little Missouri town of 'Possum Hollow. Anxious-looking men and women, with old shawls over their heads, gazed in a half-dazed fashion at the devouring machine that buzzed wickedly and puffed steam spitefully at them.

Uncle Ephram bore it as long as he could, and then took it upon himself to act as spokesman for his wronged people and himself.

"I'se done sawed an' split cordwood for the jedge for ten year, and I hain't never heerd no complaint befo' you all kim in heah," he said, addressing the mighty magnate who managed the steam and blew the shrill whistle for the sole purpose of startling the natives and impressing them with his importance.

"No, I reckon not, Uncle. You see as long as you was the best they c'd git, the people had to put up with you. But it was mighty wearin' on the nerves to have a saw screechin' in the back yard all winter, and when I come along and offered to bite it up for them and be out of the way in half a day, they saw the p'int.''

Uncle Ephram did not, and he had no ready argument with which to answer the machinist. But he knew that something was wrong. Year after year he had counted upon reducing the judge's generous woodpile, and thereby earning his livelihood. Autumn after autumn and winter after winter he had come regularly, in fair weather and in foul, to saw and split, with his grandsons, Joe and Ben, to "tote" and pile up. He carried his old-fashioned double-edged axe over his shoulder now. He picked it up from long habit when he saw his people going up the street, and joined them to see what was going on. It balanced better than any axe he had ever swung and made a cleaner cut. He handled it as an artist would his violin. Little Ben sat astride the saw-buck and watched the puffing engine with wide open eyes. Joe carried the saw.

"Howdy, Uncle, howdy," began the judge, cheerfully. "Does the work in great shape, doesn't it?" nodding toward the buzzing saw. But without waiting for an answer, he hurriedly continued: "I reckon you are 'most too old to

tackle my big woodpile another winter, Uncle.
Too hard on your rheumatism.''

Silence, and then hesitatingly: "Least ways
I reckon I kin git the job of splittin' it up for you
all, Jedge?''

"Well, you see, it's this way.   It takes three
hands to feed, besides the engineer.   And they
have to be up to their business, too.   Just any
man the boss might pick up couldn't do the work
and make it pay.   And then, the main object of
the whole thing being to get the wood out of the
way and ready for winter use, they have four
likely boys to follow the machine, and they split
and pile it before you can say Jack Robinson.''

"Yas, sah! yas, sah,'' said Uncle Eph, as he
shifted his weight to the other foot.   It never
occurred to him to "controvert'' with his betters

At every one of the houses whose occupants
were sufficiently well-to-do or fore-handed to lay
in a winter's supply of wood, he was told the
same story.   The owner of the steam machine
had visited them all and solicited their patron-
age before he decided to come to the village.   By
the time Uncle Eph had gone to each of these
ten or twelve places he realized the enormity of
the combine and was cast down utterly.

He went home to his cabin, and told his

Tottering to Its Fall.

troubles to the life-long partner of his joys and sorrows. But she had no solution to offer. She had heard her Mammy an' Ole Miss tell about about when the cotton gin and the steam thrasher came into Tennessee long time ago, but they "didn't make no sich panic as this," she "reckoned."

"Hooh! that was in slavery times, chile, when black people didn't have no need to go huntin' for work. Dem times we all was found in braid an' meat an' close an' even med' cine when we fell sick. But times is changed, ole woman, don' you 'preciate dat? Times is changed sence we was young. De good ole times is passin' away, and 'pears lak de 'struction of de worl' am comin'."

*   *   *   *   *   *   *   *   *

Towards the last of December, we had occasion to take a long ride through the oak woods. Some of the many varieties were stripped bare and their angled skeletons were etched against the grey sky, while here and there were clumps of jack oak whose leaves held on, and rattled and shivered in the wind. It was as bleak a scene as a country that is a paradise in summer could well be transformed into.

Suddenly, as we turned a shoulder of the lit-

tle Ozark mountain, we saw a plume of blue
smoke curling up over the hillside. Anyone who
is familiar with a hill region knows that there is
no sight so cheery, so suggestive of home comfort. It may come from the rude stone fireplace
and chimney of a log cabin; in truth, it could
come from no other kind of a habitation in this
particular region, for there is no other, but it is
a welcome and beautiful sight. We turned towards it, for it meant warmth, at least, and it
was the first sign of life that we had seen in many
miles. An old black man stood beside the fire,
stretching his thin hands to the blaze. In an
instant we saw that it was Ephram.

"I done clar to Mercy! Whar 'd you all come
frum?" he exclaimed. "I never took a step
out 'n my tracks to see who it was a-comin' down
the hill, jes' natchelly 'sposin it was some o' the
hill people, and they aint pertickerly anxious to
pass howdy wid an' ole niggah lak me. They 's
all po' white trash, and in reason they 'spises the
niggahs. Nevah owned a niggah in their life,
an' not much o' nothin' else. They 's just natchelly quare, 'sides bein' ornery."

All this in deference to our ignorance of the
conditions of life round about 'Possom Hollow.

It is a region in which the trees are cut as

soon as they are large enough to " square a tie."
The sparse population subsists almost exclusive-
ly by making and selling railroad ties, as it has
done for half a century, so that the industry has
become hereditary.   But it belongs by tradition
and pre-emption to the whites.   They took it up
in slavery time, long before the negroes of the
south went about seeking employment of their
own free will, and there are almost no black people in the hill country.   Uncle Ephram was an
interloper and evidently knew it, for he went on
to say: "I 'se done moved twict since I kim down
heah in Novembah, an' I 'spect I 'se got to be
pullin' out agin soon.   They all looks crossways
at me—me and Ben.   I done lef' the othah
youngstah to tote washin' back and fo'th and
split wood for his gran'-mammy, but Joe kim
along to holp me.   He 's right peart, too; built
the shack mos'ly all hisself out'n bark an' these
heah big scads we splits off squarin' ties.   Heah
he comes now.   Joe, stir up the fire.   The gem-
man an' his lady is goin' to 'light and git warm.
I 'se powerful sorry I ain't got no coffee to offer
you all, but I is got a bit o' bacon, and Joe kin
mighty soon stir up a Johnny-cake.   I reckon you
all nevah et no Johnny-cake baked in the
ashes?"

When we were ready to say good-bye, my companion asked who owned the land on which old Ephram was cutting ties.

"Oh, hit 's Ole Marse's plantation, but in law it belongs to Young Marse Tom now, I reckon."

"And did he give permission to cut ties here?"

"No, sah! No, sah! Nevah axed him, sah! Ef my ole marster, layin' in his grave, knowed dat Ephum done been run out'n town wid a monstah machine what bites up all de cord wood and grabbles de braid out 'n de ol' black man's mouf at de same time, he would jes' tuhn ovah an' say: 'Ephum, go 'long down in de oak woods an' cut ties, an' welcome. I jes' bruk loose an' kim. Hit was the onlies' thing t 'do.''

CPSIA information can be obtained
at www.ICGtesting.com
Printed in the USA
BVOW03*2249170917
495139BV00007B/61/P